Suicide and the Surviving Spirit

True Life Stories of Healing Through Mediumship

Suicide and the Surviving Spirit

True Life Stories of Healing
Through Mediumship

BECS SAWYER

Disclaimer

The statements made by the author and any recommendations of services in this book are not intended to diagnose, treat, cure or prevent any disease. The information provided and knowledge and experiences shared by the author are not intended to be a substitute for professional medical advice, diagnosis, or treatment.

ISBN 978-1-917288-996

Edited by Elaine Harrison
Cover image design by Victoria Burton
Interior design by Damian Keenan
This book was typeset in Adobe Garamond Pro and Calluna Sans
with ITC Century Std Book Condensed used as a display typeface.

To find out more about Becs, visit her website
https://becs-medium.com/

Contents

Disclaimer and Permissions

ALL STORIES AND PERSONAL ACCOUNTS included in this book have been shared with the explicit permission of the individuals involved. Names, where included, are used with the consent of those who contributed their experiences. Some names have been changed. We extend our deepest gratitude to everyone who courageously opened their hearts and allowed their stories to be shared. Their generosity and honesty have made this book possible.

This book is intended to share experiences and provide insight into the journeys of those who have lost loved ones to suicide and found comfort through spiritual mediumship.

The content is not intended as a substitute for professional medical, psychological, or therapeutic advice. If you or someone you know is struggling with mental health or experiencing suicidal thoughts, please seek support from qualified professionals or contact a helpline in your area.

The author and publisher make no guarantees about the spiritual or metaphysical concepts discussed in this book. The experiences and messages described are deeply personal and may not reflect every reader's beliefs or experiences. Readers are encouraged to approach the content with an open mind and draw their own conclusions.

While every effort has been made to ensure accuracy, the author and publisher accept no responsibility for errors, omissions, or any outcomes resulting from the application of the material contained herein. This book is a work of non-fiction based on personal experiences, and any resemblance to other events or individuals, living or deceased, is purely coincidental.

Should you need support or further guidance, please refer to the list of helplines and resources provided at the end of the book.

Dedication

THIS BOOK IS DEDICATED, firstly, to anyone and everyone who has had their world rocked to its very core by losing someone they love to suicide. My hope is that this little book might shine a guiding light on your journey.

Secondly, I dedicate this book to the courageous and brave souls who have shared their stories and experiences, for without them, there would have been no book.

Foreword

"Rebecca has been a much-cherished trainee of mine for more than a decade. Her devotion and persistence to developing her mediumship to its level of excellence is a thing of awe. I'm beyond proud and delighted that she is chronicling 'some' of her experiential reflections upon a subject still so sensitive, still so taboo, as a printed support to those in deep need for such insight, perspective, and direction.

The book's content is heartfelt healing at its best, because of the courageous and sincere sharings of the bereaved loved-one's personal testimonies. There's strength and spiritual sustenance in every chapter."

Eamonn G Downey
International Lecturer and Author

Introduction

RIGHT FROM THE START, I want to make it clear to you, the reader, that I am not a qualified therapist, nor do I possess a deep knowledge of the complexities surrounding suicide. My work is centered on reuniting those in Spirit with their loved ones who remain in the physical world.

Whatever your beliefs, I simply ask you to keep an open mind as you read these experiences and draw your own conclusions. Personally, I have absolute faith in Spirit, which I see as the ultimate intelligence, filled with unconditional love.

Of all the topics a medium could explore, suicide is perhaps the most profound. The word itself resonates deeply, evoking intense emotions, pain, heartache, and often, many unanswered questions. In this little book, I aim to share with you some of the reunions I have been privileged to facilitate between loved ones in Spirit and those still here. My hope is that this will offer some potential for healing to those who have encountered the tragedy of suicide and provide insight into my world for those drawn to read this book.

I prefer not to use the word "suicide." Instead, I use the phrase "taking themselves home," as it better encapsulates the essence of their decision—a choice to leave the earthly journey behind and return to the spiritual realm when life becomes too unbearable.

In my mediumship practice, I see instances of individuals "taking themselves home" in three distinct ways.

The first group consists of those whose lifestyle choices, such as excessive drinking, drug use, or reckless behavior, inadvertently lead to their departure from the physical world—a self-destructive cycle they couldn't escape from.

The second group includes those who make a sudden, impulsive decision driven by intense emotions, such as anger or despair. This can be an "out of the blue" event that feels so out of character when it happens.

Finally, there are those who, overwhelmed by emotional, mental, or physical pain, see "taking themselves home" as a release from their suffering. While these categories offer some insight, every case is unique.

Ultimately, my role as a medium is to facilitate healing, providing comfort and a small degree of solace to those who seek it. I believe it is important to introduce you to mediumship—what it is, how I believe it works, and why it can be a wonderful process to support those who have lost someone who has "returned home" to the loving world of Spirit, especially through suicide.

This book is not about me, "Becs the medium." As soon as I can, I want to hand over the book to those who matter most: the people who have shared their experiences with me and my work.

My hope is that as you read this book and share in the stories of these brave and wonderful people who have opened their hearts to you, allowing you to feel their pain and grief, you might also come to understand that no matter the pain of loss, love is eternal. When it comes down to it, love is all there is—the power of love. This power flows through all of us; *it* always has, and through its compassion, has the potential to heal many wounds.

For me, this is where my work truly happens—within the power of eternal love. The reunions that manifest, the coming together of loved ones, the healing, the release of suffering, and the letting go of guilt and anger all help take small steps forward from the pain of losing someone who has died by suicide.

No spiritual medium can ever take away the pain of missing a loved one, but mediumship can help shape and change how we grieve. With suicide, there are often many unanswered questions, along with emotions such as guilt, intense pain, anger, and rage, that can last a lifetime. The healing potential of mediumship through a sensitive and loving reunion can help bring some closure, allowing for the release of emotions and a movement away from the darkness of carried pain.

What is Mediumship?

LET'S LOOK AT IT LIKE THIS... Imagine a mobile phone, nothing special, just a basic mobile phone. What do you need to do to use it? Well, you obviously need to unpack it, charge the battery, insert a SIM card to connect to your favorite network, and finally, turn it on and wait for a call. Then, it's up to you to answer when it rings.

That's exactly how I work. I am simply a mobile phone. My role, each and every time, is to prepare myself, get out of the way, and be that "mobile phone" that allows the calls—the reunions. We are all mobile phones; we can all be our own mediums. But that is a topic for another book!

Mediumship is easy—it's a natural phenomenon. The physical mind of the medium, with all its chatter, is what gets in the way. Whenever I teach, the first thing I ask any student is, "How are you? What do you need to help quieten down that overthinking, rational mind?" It is only when the medium can quieten their mind and emotions that they can move on to blending with Spirit.

To explain a little deeper: for me, preparation is key, just like setting up that mobile phone. Without it, there are no "calls." The first thing I do is set the intention that I will be working, usually in the afternoon before an evening session. As I get ready and drive to the venue, my mind focuses more and more on the night ahead, and I play music that resonates with my soul in the car. Once I arrive, I follow a regular routine to attune myself.

This involves building up my working power (charging the battery), blending with the energy of those at the venue, and creating a healing space for Spirit to work in—a place of love and memories (inserting the SIM card)—and finally tuning into Spirit (turning the phone on). At that point, I'm ready for whatever the night may bring.

My role during the evening is to get myself out of the way so Spirit can do their job. I set up the space and the presence for Spirit to use. Spirit knows their job—they are the ultimate intelligence. The more I can stay out of the way, the less interference there is from my conscious mind, just like maintaining a better signal when using that mobile phone.

How does my Mediumship work?

EVERY MEDIUM IS UNIQUE, shaped by their own life experiences and their developing relationship with Spirit, which is reflected in their way of working. Almost everyone reading this has probably heard the term "clairvoyance." It's an umbrella term used extensively by many mediums and means "clear seeing." This can refer to a medium seeing Spirit either physically in front of them or in their mind's eye. It is one of the "Clairs," which include clear seeing, clear hearing, clear smelling, clear sensing, and clear knowing.

However, I can't really comment on clairvoyance because I am not a clairvoyant medium. Honestly, if I ever saw a fully manifested spirit standing in front of me, I'd probably be the first one running for the door!

I work through sensing, which develops into a feeling and then becomes a knowing—this is commonly known as clairsentience. I get to know the Spirit, meeting them in that place of love and memories, and then I can represent them, narrate, and share their story. I know we are all divine beings of the light, but Spirit will always start the reunion with you in the way you knew them. Your loved ones know what they want to share, how they want to share it, and, most importantly, where the healing, release, and love are needed for you. My passion, my role, and my greatest joy is to be that mobile phone, to facilitate those reunions but not to be involved with them—because they are yours to embrace, enjoy, and remember.

Who is Becs?

I'LL KEEP THIS SHORT—just to give you a little insight into "Becs' World." I'm not one of those mediums who have seen spirits from an early age. In fact, when I was very young, my obsession was wanting to be a mermaid! If I'm honest, that desire is still there somewhere.

As I grew, my love for all things spiritual increased. I remember, long before the internet, going to the library to look for books to read… back then, there wasn't much available. I remember watching Doris Stokes (a very well-known medium at the time) and wanting to do what she was doing, but I always got nothing… nada… zero. I sat in a few development circles but still got very little.

It was only as I went through my own physical and emotional transitions later in life that my consciousness started to flourish and find its place. And as if by magic—or rather, through perfect synchronicities—the right tutors, courses, and mentor came into my life.

Now, after years and years of personal exploration (and that's exactly what a medium is doing as they develop), I find myself in a place where my work is my life—the reason why I am on this planet in this lifetime.

Why me, and why this book?

AS A YOUNG TRANS CHILD (who thought they were the only one in the world), I spent much of my life questioning my place, growing up in fear of being discovered. The profound fear of ridicule and rejection was a constant companion. Only later in life did I find peace and gratitude for this gift we call our body.

Although I never attempted to take myself home, it has left me with a deep empathy, compassion, and understanding for those who do. I can blend with them, feel their love, and hopefully represent them and the healing they bring.

Introducing the
Voices of Healing

BEFORE I INTRODUCE these very special people and hand this book over to them, I want to thank them once more. Not only are they the reason why this book has been brought into existence, but through sharing their stories, they might help others on their own healing journey.

Each of them has had their world rocked to the very core by losing someone to suicide, and I cannot express enough my admiration and love for every one of them.

I wanted to ask the same sort of questions to each person I spoke to, in the hope that common emotions and experiences might emerge. So, I prepared a gentle questionnaire to use as a guideline.

Kirsty –
Reuniting with Billy

This wonderful lady lost her husband and has trusted me to share her story.

Why did you decide to come and see me and experience my work?

The very first time I came to see you was at Mac's Bar in Essex. The event had popped up on my Facebook wall and was scheduled for the day of the anniversary of my husband's passing. I saw this as a sign and brought my daughter along with me.

Did you come along with any hopes, wishes, or fears?

Yes, I was hoping and praying to connect with my husband, but I didn't have any fear. I've never feared spirits and was always intrigued by mediumship.

What did you feel was the pull to come to see me?

It's hard to describe, but it was an intense feeling. I just felt that somehow, for some reason, I was meant to see your event and that I was supposed to attend that night. The inner pull was so strong.

What were you searching for?

I suppose I was searching for confirmation that our soul or spirit does go somewhere after our body passes away. I was also hoping for answers from my husband—to know he was okay and if he had any message or advice for me and our children.

May I ask how you were coping and feeling up to this point?

I don't think I was coping that well, to be honest, but that's perfectly understandable. I was receiving a lot of love and support from family and friends, as well as medication for depression and attending a support group. I was just going through the motions of everyday life.

How was the evening for you?

That first evening was both exciting and emotional. It was a very busy night, and my daughter and I sat at the bar when we arrived. As you passed us, you said hello. I just thought you were friendly and asked if we'd been before. I didn't know you were Becs. My jaw nearly hit the floor when the event started, and you walked down to the front.

How has it helped?

It has helped me immensely with my healing journey. I had a connection that first night and several since. It has helped me come to terms with his loss, and now I have a greater understanding and awareness of his presence and the signs that he is still around us. I've also gained more knowledge and understanding about suicide and feel that the stigma and trauma have significantly reduced for me.

What was it like experiencing the reunion?

Being reunited with my husband through you was an amazing experience. It has brought me so much comfort to know that he is aware of just how much he is loved and missed and that we still have the love and connection, even though he's not physically here. The emotions during our connection were overwhelming—the tears, love, and laughter—I will always cherish them.

How did I come to you?

You started to describe my late husband—his personality, mannerisms, character, and traits, including some of the funny things he said and did. You made that connection, and we both knew it was for us. When you said he wouldn't want to own how he passed, that was exactly him.

What were you feeling as we started working together?

I felt great excitement when we connected and couldn't wait to hear more. However, I did feel anxious and nervous that first time, as I didn't know how others in the room would think or feel regarding the suicide due to the stigma and ignorance I had come across from people previously. You were so sensitive and compassionate in the way you worked with him that I lost that awful feeling and fear about what others might be thinking.

How was the reunion for you?

It was truly amazing. I could literally feel his presence in the room—I could feel his energy. My daughter and I both knew it was him, and we loved that you brought him through exactly as he was and didn't change him one little bit.

Has this helped in any way with feelings of anger, guilt, or loss?

Yes, it has definitely helped. Death by suicide is so complex and unlike any other loss. It leaves you overwhelmed with emotions, unanswered questions, confusion, and no closure. Then you have the pain, anger, guilt, and constant "what ifs."

Through connecting with him and learning about suicide loss, I have learned to process these feelings and gain some inner peace, allowing me to let go of these feelings and giving me the safe space to grieve.

And following the night, have you felt any shift, change, or healing within you?

After a reunion, I try to remember all the details to relay to our children. I then feel like my mind and body are much calmer and more relaxed. It feels like it's allowing me to let go of the turmoil in my mind and release the trauma within my body. I have shifted from surviving to thriving.

What would you say to another person or family experiencing the same thing?

Firstly, I would express my deepest sympathy for their loss. I would let them know that everything they are feeling, thinking, and experiencing is completely normal and that they are not alone. I would encourage them to stay hydrated, eat, and rest, be kind and gentle with themselves, and seek the comfort and support they need from family, friends, and professionals. Don't make any major decisions or changes if you don't need to—there's no rush. There's no right or wrong; the experience is different for everyone.

Is there anything you would like to share that would help anyone else dealing with a loved one taking their own life?

This is a difficult one; grief and healing are individual. I can only share my experience. I would say you're not alone—reach out, take an active role in your healing journey in a healthy way, whatever that looks like for you. Below are some things I've tried and still continue:

- Meditation, yoga, gym
- Walking, reading, music
- Joining a support group
- Attending church
- Engaging in hobbies
- Living in the present
- Practicing breathing and mindfulness
- Taking time for myself and social time
- Medication and therapy

As you can see, the list can be endless and different for everyone. I personally find that lots of little things help me.

Keeley –
Reuniting with Nick

Such a brave soul and warrior who lost her very best friend. Her story is one of incredible fortitude and healing.

Why did you decide to come and see me and my work?

I've always been intrigued and curious about the unconscious mind, the world of Spirit, and what happens to our souls when we die. I had seen you on a couple of occasions at various venues and, during those times, had witnessed your genuine and unique connection to Spirit and the accuracy you often achieve within your readings for people, particularly at Mac's Bar. It was a very last-minute decision to come and see you that evening after I had decided earlier that day that my suicidal feelings, relating to the complex trauma I had endured during my childhood, were totally winning the war inside my head, and I wanted to end my life. However, I felt I needed to try and check in first with my best friend who had passed away, also by suicide, a couple of years before. I messaged and asked if tickets were available earlier in the day and was told they weren't. Then, about two hours before the show, a ticket became available.

Did you come along with any hopes, wishes, or fears?

Having prepped things over the weekend, I was feeling totally overwhelmed, lost, and empty, and needing a miracle to save my life. I was hoping for direction and insight from my missing piece in life—my best friend, Nick. He was the person who always got me and understood me the most after we had both endured appalling and incredibly tough childhoods.

We always talked for hours; we knew everything about each other and built each other up when others tried to bring us down. His extraordinary energy and sense of humor meant he could make me belly laugh even on the days I was unsure if I would ever smile again. Nick inconceivably took his own life a few years ago on a day I will never forget. He left not knowing what an amazing soul he was and how much of an impact he made on my life.

On the night I came to your show, I needed my soulmate, my protector—the one I had trusted with my life—to tell me if I should stay here in this world or go. Just before your show, I sat in my car with a box of different medications, all in a blue and white box I was going to use later that night, and found myself saying, "If you come through for me tonight and tell me no, then I won't do it." So, absolutely no pressure then, Becs!

What did you feel was the pull to come to see me?

I've been to several of your evenings and seen the impact of your connections and reunions and the healing your messages have had on others. Nick, despite being so loud, was a very private person with a keen interest in spirituality, and he would have loved your personality, honesty, and the way you present things. You would have loved his energy and silly sense of humor. If he was going to come through to anyone, it would be you.

May I ask how you were coping and feeling up to this point?
I knew at the time I had many positive things in my life to live for, including my work, family, and good friends, but I was also having intensive counseling and therapy, covering some really hard issues. No matter how hard I tried or what calming strategies I used, I didn't feel I had the energy to be strong anymore—a tiredness that all the sleep in the world would never fix.

What was it like experiencing the reunion?
I don't really remember any of the other readings or messages that came through that night as my mind was elsewhere. But from the moment you spoke about someone who wouldn't usually come through and whose connection was so strong and full of love but with a companion connection, I had no choice but to listen and put up my hand.

What were you feeling as we started working together?

I was incredibly nervous and wanted to hide but quickly reminded myself of why I had come along in the first place. Within seconds, you affirmed it was definitely Nick, providing details of his passing and taking great care in how you approached delivering his messages and addressing the struggles he had previously had, including specific details regarding how I had stockpiled medication and even the type and color of the box it was in.

How was the reunion for you?

It's immensely therapeutic to know that our loved ones still have life on the other side and watch us as closely as if they were still by our side, which I often felt anyway. During the reunion, you provided me with spot-on evidence not only about Nick and why he needed to take his own life but also the events that were impacting my life at that time. During the reading, you checked in with both Nick and me to ensure we felt comfortable continuing, providing genuine empathy and support. I was in tears almost immediately as the reunion began, especially after hearing that Nick only stayed on this side for as long as he did because of our friendship. I then received the answer to the most burning question I had: that tonight wasn't my time to die!

You said how he knew I was planning to take my own life that very night and made me promise him I would not do it.

How has it helped?

It has honestly made such a huge impact on my life. I wouldn't have had a life without the reunion and your time afterwards. When those thoughts enter my mind now, like they do every so often, I take myself back to that night and remind myself it's not my time.

I have always felt a sense of guilt about Nick's passing, wishing I had done more and sought help for him sooner, but rationally, I know and recognize it was his personal choice to do what he did. The way in which he did it meant it wasn't just a cry for help—he needed to go. Hearing directly from him that his always-busy mind is now at peace is really comforting.

And following the night, have you felt any shift, change, or healing within you?

I can say with 100% honesty that I believe your connection to Nick and our conversation and hug after others had left that night saved my life. I will be forever grateful that your acceptance and understanding made me feel safe enough to hand you all of the pills I had planned on taking and for your continued support and guidance during my healing journey. I still have a long way to go, but I'm going, and that counts for something.

What would you say to another person or family experiencing the same thing?

For someone thinking of suicide, take time to remind the parts of you that are scared that there are also parts of you that are incredibly brave. It will be difficult to take in when feeling suicidal, but the feelings you have at that time are often temporary, and you may not always feel like that.

The very first step to saving your life starts with reaching out, which is incredibly scary to do but takes some of that huge weight off your shoulders.

Rebecca-Louise –
Reuniting with Tim

Rebecca-Louise lost her very special brother, Tim. This is a unique story of a reunion that began even before he fully transitioned into Spirit, while he was still physically present in what I want to respectfully call a dream-like state. He could no longer verbally communicate or control his physical body.

To give a little more background to this truly unique and incredible display of spiritual intelligence: I have on occasion experienced Spirit working with me before someone has fully left their physical body, particularly with those experiencing advanced dementia or Alzheimer's, those on life support, and in this case, Tim.

I believe this can happen because, as the physical body and brain start to lose their gentle grip on the soul, the soul finds space to expand and "be free," if only for a short while. For me, it is a beautiful experience.

Why did you decide to come and see me and my work?

I didn't attend one of your shows, but my brother's friend Lucy did. Lucy has been to your shows quite a few times, and during one of them, Tim came through. She instantly knew it was him. She got in touch with my mum, who then contacted you and said, "I think Tim came through in one of your shows. Would you like to meet him? Because he's still here."

That's when you came down to the neurological unit he was in, and we met in the sensory garden. He was in his chair, and the very first message that came through was about my boyfriend's Spurs shirt and what a s**t team they are.

I can still clearly remember the venue where this happened. I was taken straight to the people in the front row (this is known as "going direct"). As I shared the reunion, the lady receiving the messages said, "But he's still here."

At first, this seemed confusing, but as she explained that Tim was in a deep state of physical detachment, it all slipped into place. I was able to explain what I believed was happening—that Tim's soul was expanding and reaching out before his full transition to Spirit.

What was that like for you?

That was mad because he couldn't talk at all. It was surreal because he was in a dream-like state. He was communicating with you, Becs, about the Spurs shirt, and my mum received some information via you too. But at that point, he became frustrated.

I remember he tried to communicate more deeply, and when he couldn't get through as he wanted to, he started sulking.

I could feel it. He went completely quiet.

You asked my mum, "Does he sulk?" and she said, "Oh, he's the worst sulker ever!" That was when everything clicked into place for us. You only met Tim the one time in person, but it was such a profound experience.

Tim then passed sometime later.

What happened after his passing?

After the funeral, we came to one of your evenings, where he came through again—you said, "like a steam train."

This time, he mentioned something about his guitar being broken. You said you were confused, Becs, because you'd seen the guitar standing at his funeral. But the guitar had indeed been broken (the headstock had broken off), and he had been upset about this, but we got it repaired. No one could play it like Tim did. It was his absolute favorite, and you could feel the grooves where his fingers used to play.

You told us how much having the guitar at the funeral meant to him. No one outside the immediate family knew about the broken headstock, yet you mentioned it, which was another turning point for us.

There was also an extremely personal message that came through that we cannot share here.

Was there anything else that stood out from the reunions?

Yes. He also came through with a message about a 50-pence piece he had given to my dad, dated 1969. My dad carried that coin everywhere with him, in the back of his phone case. Tim mentioned the coin and what it symbolized, and my dad was completely comforted by that.

It was the same with the story about the fishing in Belgium—he came through with a joke about who had caught the bigger fish. It was those little details that only our family knew, which reassured us that he was still around.

How did these experiences help you with your grief?

The first time I came to one of your shows after Tim had passed, I didn't know what to expect. I had always believed in the possibility of communication, but I had never lost someone so close before.

Tim was the first real loss I experienced, and I never imagined he would actually come through. But when he did, it was such validation. It gave me hope and comfort that even though he's not here physically anymore, I know he's still around me.

Coming to your shows has helped me navigate my grief, helped with acceptance of what's happened, and shown that the love is still unconditional.

Do you enjoy watching and listening to other people's reunions?

I love it. Watching the other reunions at your shows is also very healing. You can see how much it means to people to hear from their loved ones. Sometimes, they come along so desperate to hear from their loved ones to help navigate their own grief—they are hoping for connection and reassurance. And when you see that happen, it's lovely. For example, there was a mother who came through for her granddaughter. She had so much love for the granddaughter but had never really given the mum the time of day. Then, when you started to work with her, it really helped and gave her that closure. You could see it on her face—it gave her the validation she needed to make peace with things.

You could feel the energy shift as she finally started to make peace with things.

Has experiencing so many reunions helped you personally?

These experiences have helped me so much. I had a lot of frustration, anger, and upset. Losing Tim felt so unfair—no one knows when their time will come, but it was too soon. Tim was my best friend—there were only 18 months between us—and I was so angry and hurt, but I needed to let that go.

Understanding that when he's crossed over, all of that hurt and suffering is gone helped me. Knowing he's at peace now gave me comfort and helped me accept what's happened. That's been the healing for me through coming to your shows.

What would you say to someone else who loses someone through suicide?

I would tell anyone going through something similar that while you can't change what's happened—sure, you can sit there and scream and ask 'why'—you have to make peace with it. You have to understand that it was their choice with all the hurt and everything they were going through.

Once you start to understand that, you can make peace with it. Knowing that your loved one is no longer suffering, that they are at peace, and that the love between you is unconditional and will never go away is crucial. It's important to make peace with it yourself because if you don't, it can eat you up inside. I would suggest going to a mediumship night because even listening to other people's reunions gives you that sense of comfort.

Finally, I've learned there's no one to blame for what happened. It's ultimately a choice they made, and it really does hurt, but it's not your fault. You cannot blame yourself. We were initially full of what-ifs: 'What if we had done this or that?' You might feel guilty, thinking you could have done something differently, but you did everything you could. You'll never get over losing someone you love, but you can learn to live with it and find a new way forward—to navigate a new life. I truly believe Tim wouldn't want me to sit here feeling sad and hurting—he'd want me to remember the good times and live my life fully.

Claire –
Reuniting with Steve

Claire is a dear friend of mine, whose partner Steve (whom I also knew) died by suicide. Claire works within the spiritual world, and I'm so pleased she wanted to share her experiences and her wise words.

How did I help you during this time?

"My experience with you and Steve wasn't limited to a demonstration setting. The way you really helped me when Steve passed was through the online meditation sessions. They allowed me to connect with him in Spirit, which was a great comfort and also confirmation of his life beyond this realm."

What fears did you have about his passing?

"I think that those left behind after a loved one dies by suicide often fear that because they have taken their own life and haven't died from natural causes, their soul may not be at rest. Having a medium confirm that your loved one has not only passed over to a peaceful place but is also able to provide evidence that they are still with you in your everyday life is a real gift."

How did his passing affect you?

"Suicide is a shocking and abrupt way to lose a loved one, even if, as in my case, the person has been in a severe and chronic troubled mental or emotional state. Again, the connection a medium provides is invaluable in softening that shock, and having you in close proximity was very reassuring and calming for me."

Can you share a specific experience?

"In terms of actually coming to one of your demonstrations and connecting with Steve that way, the one I probably remember the most was at The Shed. It was very interesting because Steve brought through another Steve, who had also died by suicide and was the late partner of my sister's friend who was sitting next to me!"

"It was a really powerful experience with a lot of crossover between the two of them, but also some very specific evidence given that was individual to them both. I think it really confirmed to me that Steve is doing what he promised to do, which was to help other souls that choose to cross over the way he did."

How has your spiritual background influenced your journey?

"Because I have been on a spiritual, energetic, and mediumistic journey myself, I was quite at peace with Steve's journey. But it really helped with processing the emotion and the physical absence of him to have confirmation of his eternal presence from another person. I remain eternally grateful to you."

Hilary —
Reuniting with her Sister

Hilary, who lost her sister when she was still a teenager.

Why did you decide to come to see me for my work?

I had heard great things about you, and honestly, once I heard that, I thought I had to come to an evening.

Did you have any hopes or fears when you came along?

I think there's always a hope that someone will come through.

How had you been coping up to this point?

I was actually doing OK. I had reached a place of acceptance about where she is, thanks in large part to all the healing work I had done for myself over the years since she had passed.

Can you describe your experience during your reunion?

I remember it well. You said you were finished, but then you felt compelled to do one last reading. At first, you talked about my friend Kate, who had passed from cancer. You described her so beautifully, and I hadn't heard from her since she passed, maybe 18 months ago. Then you mentioned my sister, how she had passed, and then brought her in alongside my friend.

You described her so clearly and shared memories of her, and it gave me so much comfort. It felt like a confirmation that everything I believed was true. When you mentioned my sister was there with her, I was filled with joy, knowing they were together. They were best friends in life, and it brought me so much comfort.

How did that make you feel?
It was emotional but filled with happiness, knowing they were safe and together. It confirmed everything I had imagined and hoped.

Have you noticed any shifts or changes in yourself since that reunion?
Yes, definitely. I feel a deeper connection to my own developing mediumship now. I can distinguish between what's in my head and what is genuinely them coming through.

What advice would you give to someone experiencing a similar situation?
Time really is the greatest healer. You may not believe it at first, but it's true. Patience is key. I spent years trying to get a message from my sister, and when I finally did, it was from the right medium. It's all about timing and being on the right vibrational level.

Emma –
Reuniting with Ben

A brave mum who was brought to see me by a friend, hoping to connect with her son.

Why Did You Decide to Come and See Me and My Work?

Well, I've always been skeptical of anything to do with psychics or mediums or the like. A good friend, who is a firm believer in the spiritual side of life, told me all about an amazing medium she had seen. She and others had incredible spiritual experiences that helped them on their path to healing from their losses. That's when I decided to book my first night with you back in the summer.

Did You Come Along with Any Hopes, Wishes, or Fears?

I wasn't really sure what to expect, but deep down, I hoped I would be able to connect with my son. I wasn't sure if it would happen— I suppose I was still quite dubious—but I was very keen to keep an open mind. I was worried that any messages or connections that came through might be ones I wouldn't want to hear, but I think that was purely down to my own self-doubt. I also don't like to cry in public and was nervous about how I might react if my boy came through. However, I felt I had nothing to lose, and I thought that just hearing other people's messages would be both comforting and intriguing.

I was concerned that I might be too closed off to actually receive a message, but I put my faith and trust in you and your abilities.

What Drew You to See Me?

I'd say closure! Everything happened so quickly and so finally, and not getting a chance to say our goodbyes was extremely tough.
I carried a lot of self-blame around the whole situation, and although I knew deep down I wasn't at fault, I was hoping it would bring me the closure I needed.

What Were You Searching For?

I was searching for comfort and hope that my boy was still out there somewhere, now happy and at peace. He was a troubled soul but so loving and caring, and knowing this would bring me a sense of ease about the situation.

How Were You Coping and Feeling Up to This Point?

I was struggling mentally, blaming myself for everything and feeling like I was at a very low point in my life. I'd get upset about how quickly everything had happened, not knowing how he felt or if I was at fault. The lack of closure made such a tragic loss even harder to bear. It left a big hole in both my life and my heart.

How Was the Evening for You?

I've been to two of your nights this year, once in the summer and the other just last week! The first evening was so comforting, hearing other people's stories, experiences, and messages from their loved ones. It was an amazing experience to be a part of!

My boy came through with his message on the first night, right at the very end of the evening—fashionably late as always! You described my boy to a tee and captured his personality so well. I was in shock. I wasn't expecting him to come through, but he did. It was so comforting to hear the messages he wanted to give me. You delivered them in such a beautiful way, and I will forever be thankful for your ability to do this. The comfort was absolutely amazing. It felt like I had finally gained the closure I needed, along with the reassurance that I wasn't at fault. This has helped me process his passing a little more easily. I had been struggling to grieve properly before this—it was constantly on my mind.

My friend invited me to your next local event, and I decided to go as it had been such a lovely experience, not only for myself but also hearing other people's messages. My boy came through yet again on this second night, and I was blown away. He wasn't finished with the message he wanted to give!

Obviously, it was very emotional, but again he assured me that he was happy and that I needed to stop blaming myself and stop self-sabotaging. He knew just how much I had been beating myself up. His messages, telling me I was a good mum and a good person, meant the absolute world to me!

How Has This Helped?

It's made me feel more at ease about losing my boy. He was my stepson, but he came through to tell me he saw me as his mum. He reassured me that I did everything right and that none of it was my fault. It gave me clarity about his mindset in that moment.

It's helped me to realize that he is now at peace, and I need to be too—until we meet again. I miss him dearly and always will, but I can remember the messages he gave through you and have that closure that he's okay, along with a clearer understanding of how he felt at the end of his short life. I don't constantly blame myself anymore, as I know he wouldn't be happy with me for doing so. It's allowing me to properly grieve and understand my emotions.

What Was It Like Experiencing the Reunion?

The first time I was in a state of shock and didn't see it coming, but I was so grateful to get both the reunions with Ben. The second night I felt a warm glow just before he came through with his messages, and it was so special and comforting.

What Were You Feeling as We Started Working Together?

I was apprehensive, anxious, and intrigued by the work that you do! But I put those feelings aside and allowed myself to be open to the process. I think it's an amazing thing that you can do for people who have lost their loved ones, providing them with a special place to receive their messages.

How Was the Reunion for You?

It was emotional! I don't cry in public and was a little in shock, but I could feel it all in my stomach. I can't explain the immense comfort it gave me to hear those messages that I so desperately needed to hear. Not knowing how he was or how he felt had been making my own mental health battles even harder. The fact that you were able to describe him so well made me realize how deeply you had connected with him. He was such a special young man, and everything you said rang true.

I'm no longer skeptical of the other side. Being open to it can truly change your perspective and make you feel more at ease about a horrible situation. Death is never easy, but when it's a young person, it's even more difficult. The messages felt like a warm hug, and I deeply appreciate the hugs you gave me too.

Has This Helped with Anger, Guilt, or Loss?

Most definitely! Even now, I still find myself blaming myself, but

I have to think back to what you've said. I retrain my brain when it wanders because I know he wouldn't want me to keep blaming myself. I used to be angry at myself often, but now I feel at peace. I know I did my best for him, and he's no longer hurting—that's the most important thing for me. Knowing he's no longer suffering from everything that was going on in his head brings me so much comfort. It's like he's sitting on my shoulder, reassuring me that everything is okay.

Have You Felt Any Shift, Change, or Healing Since the Reunion?

Absolutely, the guilt has been lifted, and even if it sounds cliché, I know he's always still with me! I'm able to process everything more clearly, and it's really helped with my mental health. I can hold my head high and carry on, striving to make him proud. I no longer have that heavy weight or dark cloud hanging over me. I look out for him—my shining star in the sky, as you so warmly and lovingly described it.

What Would You Say to Someone Experiencing the Same Thing?

I would say, if you're thinking about attending an event, even if you're skeptical, give it a try and keep an open mind! I was super skeptical myself, but Bec has kept my boy's memory alive. It has brought me great peace, understanding, and immense comfort as well.

Is There Anything You Would Like to Share to Help Others?

Accept that there is a reason why these things happen. Usually, the person simply cannot continue living the way they were. Their pain was so immense that, sadly, they felt they could no longer go on. Unfortunately, the mental health system is so overstretched that not everyone can access the help they need. But please, never see this as a reflection on you!

We're not trained professionals, and we don't always see the signs. Many times, they hid their feelings so well that you wouldn't have even known they were struggling. They were possibly trying to protect you—and, like my Ben, they still are from the other side.

Seeing the right medium can help you come to terms with why they felt the need to leave. It can bring you comfort and peace. Losing someone close, especially to suicide, is one of the toughest paths to walk, but I've learned that self-blame doesn't help, and no one is to blame

I have so much respect for Bec's work. It can completely change your mindset around the situation and help bring you that inner peace. If it's something that interests you, I strongly encourage you to approach it with an open mind.

Remember, your loved ones live on in your heart and mind. Take it easy on yourself.

Final Reflections:
Memories of Reuniting Loved Ones

THIS FINAL CHAPTER comes from me, Becs. I want to share a few of my most meaningful memories from the times I've been privileged to reunite loved ones who have passed through suicide with those left behind.

For those who know me, they'll be familiar with my truly shocking memory—often described as being like that of a goldfish! I only seem to remember moments from my work with Spirit if they contribute to my growth as a medium or have some future significance. That said, here are some recollections that have stayed with me, and I hope they provide further insight into the profound topic of this book.

No Such Thing as Hell

There is often a stigma and condemnation attached to those who die by suicide. In fact, suicide was still illegal in the UK until 1961, and many people mistakenly believe that the Bible condemns individuals who take their own lives to Hell. However, the Bible says no such thing; this is a common misconception.

This topic arose one night when I was working at a family and friends group event. A man approached me from Spirit. I never edit my work; my role is to give Spirit a voice. Sometimes, very raw words and feelings come through, as they did that night. This man revealed that he had murdered his wife and then gone to his place of work and taken his own life.

In front of me sat this man's sister, who had been left to raise his two children. It's not uncommon for me to swear occasionally, and at that moment, as I looked at his sister, I sent a thought to Spirit: "Just where the f**k do I go with this?"

And then, with my next breath, the words came out of my mouth: "It's OK, love. There's no such thing as Hell."

With that, this wonderful woman started to cry and said, "Everyone keeps telling me he has gone to Hell, and that is all I wanted to know."

Even in the midst of such pain, anger, and intense emotions, Spirit knew exactly what to say.

The Youngest I Ever Worked With: A Teenager

For me, losing a child must be one of the hardest things to bear. Losing a child to suicide adds a depth to the grief that words cannot describe.

One of the most poignant reunions I've ever been part of involved a young boy reconnecting with his mum. He gently reassured her of his eternal love, told her he was safe and loved, and sought to ease her overwhelming guilt and the constant questioning of what she might have done wrong.

Nothing I say or do can take away the pain of losing someone. For this grieving mum, words couldn't erase the hurt. But she later shared that the reunion brought her profound healing.

She had been haunted by the fear that her son was alone, and she longed to join him. His words—sharing that he was safe and loved in Spirit—helped ease her despair and gave her the strength to move forward.

I often say this, and I firmly believe it: no one gets stuck when they crossover. Spirit takes meticulous care with every passing. They are the ultimate intelligence, and every soul is met with unconditional love.

The Very Recent Passing

I tend to question many of the so-called "common truths" in my work. One of these is the belief about how quickly someone who has passed can connect with their loved ones.

In my experience, they can connect the very same day. No one has told them they can't!

Often, those who have recently passed will gently validate their presence. They share soft messages of love, letting their loved ones know they are safe and that life is eternal.

One such case involved a young man who had recently taken himself to the woods and passed. He reached out to his aunt during one of my events, gently sharing how he transitioned to Spirit.

I asked her, "Who is Nick? He's almost shouting!" She replied, "That's my dad."

I said, "I don't want to kill your dad off, but he's saying he is with Nick."

She smiled and explained, "Yes, my dad is in Spirit. All my family and I want to know is if he is with my dad."

The intelligence of Spirit is remarkable. This young man knew exactly what his family needed to hear, offering them comfort through his simple yet profound message.

The Angel on the Shoulder

Sometimes, Spirit shares details so specific that they provide undeniable reassurance.

One evening, a young man reunited with his mum, who was in deep despair after losing her son to suicide. He spoke to her gently, fully aware that she was on the brink of giving up on life herself.

As the reunion drew to a close, I said, "I am the angel on your shoulder."

I worried it might sound generic, but I always strive to convey Spirit's exact words.

The woman looked at me in shock, pulled down her top, and

revealed a tattoo of an angel on her shoulder, with her son's name beneath it.

Guilt Release: The Phone Call

One of the most pervasive emotions carried by those left behind after a suicide is guilt. They often wonder if they could have done more.

One evening, I facilitated a reunion between two close friends—two men who shared an unbreakable bond. The friend who had passed expressed his deep gratitude for the unwavering support his friend had given him during his struggles.

He shared, "Even if you had phoned me that night, my mind was made up."

The man sitting in front of me visibly released the burden of guilt he had carried for so long. With tears streaming down his face, he whispered, "Thank you."

Later, he told me he had planned to call his friend that night but decided to wait until morning.

Spirit always knows the exact words needed to bring healing and peace.

A Final Thought

AS YOU REACH THE END of this book, I want to thank you for joining me on this journey.

At the outset, I made it clear that I am not a professional therapist or counselor. My role is to facilitate reunions between those who have crossed into the Spirit world and those of us still navigating this physical existence.

However, following this chapter, you will find a list of support groups, helplines, and charities whose expertise is just a call away.

Thank you for allowing me to share these stories and experiences with you.

Love and Life Are Eternal

We are all made of beautiful stardust, and this life is but a flicker in our eternal existence.

Oceans of love,

Becs xx

Helplines and Charities for Suicide Support and Mental Health

BELOW IS A LIST OF HELPLINES and charities offering support for those affected by suicide, as well as individuals struggling with their mental health. Whether you're based in the UK or the USA, these organizations can provide help, guidance, and a listening ear.

United Kingdom

SAMARITANS

Website: *www.samaritans.org*
Helpline: 116 123 (free, 24/7)
Email: jo@samaritans.org
Offers confidential support to anyone in emotional distress or at risk of suicide.

CALM (CAMPAIGN AGAINST LIVING MISERABLY)

Website: *www.thecalmzone.net*
Helpline: 0800 58 58 58 (free, 5 pm to midnight, 7 days a week)
Text: Use their webchat service on their website.
Focused on preventing male suicide and providing mental health support.

MIND

Website: *www.mind.org.uk*

Helpline: 0300 123 3393 (9 am–6 pm, Monday to Friday)

Text: 86463

Offers advice and support for those experiencing mental health issues.

PAPYRUS UK

Website: *www.papyrus-uk.org*

Helpline: 0800 068 4141 (HOPELINE UK for people under 35)

Text: 07860039967

Supports young people struggling with suicidal thoughts and offers advice to those concerned about them.

CRUSE BEREAVEMENT SUPPORT

Website: *www.cruse.org.uk*

Helpline: 0808 808 1677 (free, Monday to Friday, 9 am–5 pm)

Provides specialist bereavement counselling, including support for those affected by suicide.

United States

988 SUICIDE & CRISIS LIFELINE

Website: *www.988lifeline.org*

Helpline: Dial 988 (available 24/7)

Offers free and confidential support to anyone in distress, including those affected by suicide.

CRISIS TEXT LINE

Website: *www.crisistextline.org*

Text: HOME to 741741 (available 24/7)

   Provides support for mental health crises via text message.

NATIONAL ALLIANCE ON MENTAL ILLNESS (NAMI)

Website: *www.nami.org*

Helpline: 1-800-950-NAMI (6264) (Mo to Fri 10 am–10 pm ET)

   Offers support, education, and resources for those dealing with
   mental health issues.

AMERICAN FOUNDATION FOR SUICIDE PREVENTION (AFSP)

Website: *www.afsp.org*

   Provides education, advocacy, and support for those affected
   by suicide.

THE TREVOR PROJECT

Website: www.thetrevorproject.org

Helpline: 1-866-488-7386 (available 24/7)

Text: START to 678678

   Specializes in providing crisis intervention for LGBTQ+ youth.

SAMHSA'S NATIONAL HELPLINE

Website: *www.samhsa.gov*

Helpline: 1-800-662-HELP (4357) (available 24/7)

   Free and confidential assistance for individuals and families
   facing mental health or substance use challenges.

If you or someone you know is struggling, please don't hesitate to reach out. These organizations are here to help, offering a safe space and guidance to navigate even the most difficult times.

To find out more about Becs, visit her website and social media pages:

Website: *Becs-medium.com*
Facebook: *Facebook.com/BecsUK*
Instagram: *Instagram.com/becs_spiritual_medium*
Email: *becs@becs-medium.com*

About Becs

BECS (REBECCA) SAWYER is one of Britain's most loved mediums, bringing comfort, healing, laughter, and tears to many. Becs is *clairsentient*, which means she literally feels and senses spirit, getting to know them so she can then narrate their story and help facilitate that special reunion. Her work is described by many as 'healing' — including helping heal relationships between those still alive and loved ones who have passed.

It wasn't until Becs went through her own physical and emotional transitions as a transgender woman that her mediumship truly started to unfold. She has been demonstrating mediumship for over 20 years and has a busy schedule with her mediumship nights, workshops, and unique Re-Creation readings (which have a twelve-month waiting list).

She runs regular weekly healing meditations live on her Facebook page and a monthly live evening of mediumship too.

Becs has been featured widely across the media, including an appearance on Good Morning TV.

She has a CD available called *Everyone's a Medium*, featuring gentle guided meditation exercises to help the listener blend with their own eternal soul and then with loved ones in spirit. This is now also available to listen to for FREE on SoundCloud here:

https://soundcloud.com/user-757446545.

Printed in Great Britain
by Amazon

57530901R00037